# HORSES TO FOLLOW

# FOLLOW

## 2019 FLAT SEASON

### JAKE COLCLOUGH

*AuthorHouse™ UK*
*1663 Liberty Drive*
*Bloomington, IN 47403  USA*
*www.authorhouse.co.uk*
*Phone: 0800.197.4150*

*Published by AuthorHouse 01/15/2019*

*ISBN: 978-1-7283-8188-6 (sc)*
*ISBN: 978-1-7283-8187-9 (e)*

*Print information available on the last page.*

authorHOUSE®

# Acknowledgments

Disclaimer: All information was correct at the time of printing, author nor publisher can be blamed for change of trainer or ownership.

Front Cover: Winter – Wayne Lordan, Aiden O'Brien

Photography Front Cover – Josh Pearson Photography
/ www.joshpearsonphotography.weebly.com/

**RACING POST**

**Welcome** v

K-Q    25-36

A-F     1-12

R-Z     37-50

G-J    13-24

Thank you!

# Welcome

Welcome to Horses to Follow 3-Year-Olds 2019.

The guide contains 50 horses which are entering their 3-year-old careers. Colts or fillies, potential classic winners or useful handicappers in the making; the aim of the guide is to supply you with as many winners in the 2019 season as possible.

To aid our search for winners, the book reflects upon the horses' juvenile campaigns in 2018. The horses shortlisted have been gathered based upon performances and potential.

In 2018, British Horse Racing was blessed with a thrilling crop of 3-year-old champion fillies. Alpha Centauri swept to save the mile division for Mrs John Harrington and the Niarchos family. The multi-Group 1 winning pair of fillies Sea of Class and Laurens for William Haggas and Karl Burke respectively. As well as the St Leger runner-up Lah Ti Dah, from the beautifully bred family of Oaks winner Dar Re Mi, trained by John Gosden. The difficult agenda we have on our hands, is that out of that crop of high class 3-year-olds, only 2 of them raced as juveniles. Sea of Class was a late foal, and Lah Ti Dar wasn't given her debut until April at Newmarket. However, over the course of 2018 plenty of promising juvenile performers have emerged and the guide assembles these into one place.

Now, why three-year olds? This is the most exciting year in a horses' racing career, as their potential is unfulfilled and an improving horse can be very valuable to keep onside of. For example the crop of fillies, if you backed each and every one of their runs to a £10 stake you would be £495.90 better off for it. Last season at this stage we had already seen the Guineas winner (Saxon Warrior, Aiden O'Brien) and the Derby winner (Masar, Charlie Appelby) which is encouraging enough to take a look at next year's potential.

The guide will include some of the top performers from the juvenile season but not only the superstars will make the cut, the plan is to give you a collection of 3-year-olds that will progress from their 2-year-old campaigns and hopefully have a successful year. Giving you a nice crop of winners for the coming 2019 Flat Season.

Calyx – the unbeaten son of Kingman seeks classic triumph.

# A-F

# Advertise

b c Showcasing - Furbelow (Pivotal)

Martyn Meade - Phoenix Thoroughbred Limited

A scopey sprinter trained by Martyn Meade. **Advertise** is a champion 2-year-old in his own right, he made light work of Aiden O'Brien's Sergei Prokofiev in the Phoenix Stakes, a Group 1 which O'Brien had before dominated with a record 17 wins in the event. Only found potentially classy type Calyx one too good in the Coventry, further progress in the Showcasing colt is questionable. Whether he has reached is highest mark could be quite possible but it is worth keeping him onside, especially how bullish Meade is about his ability, and if he continues to grow into his huge frame could be a force to be reckoned with in Group 1 sprints in 2019. Unlikely to get the mile but is a tough and quick individual, and Showcasing progeny tend to be versatile ground wise.

# Anthony Van Dyck

b c Galileo - Believe'N'Succeed (Exceed and Excel)

Aiden O'Brien – Derrick Smith, Mrs John Magnier and Michael Tabor

Regally bred **Anthony Van Dyck** boasts a very speedy and stamina entwined pedigree which should see him performing at middle distance in the coming year. The colt began on debut over seven furlongs which adds to the evidence that he would stay well over a mile, but with the print of Aussie sprinter Exceed and Excel on the dam's side provides that turn of foot and speed, which saw him record successes at Group 3 and 2 level over seven furlongs. He holds Derby entries and this looks like a trip that would suit (14/1). Just touched off by classy type Quorto in the National Stakes, where he battled well and will come on a lot from that once stepped up in trip.

**Anthony Van Dyck** beat 1¼ length by Godolphin's Quorto in the Goff's Vincent O'Brien National Stakes Group 1 in September.

# Breath Of Air

b c Bated Breath – Western Appeal (Gone West)

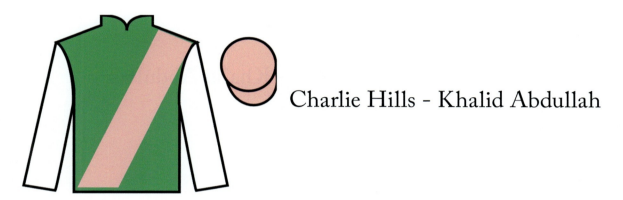

Charlie Hills - Khalid Abdullah

An interesting colt for Charlie Hills, the son of Bated Breath had no run on debut at Salisbury and didn't learn much despite travelling strongly out the back of the field; that form has worked out well with Flashcard and Dirty Rascal coming out and improving. The form was then supported by himself when he reappeared and won impressively at Newbury by 3¾ lengths, he was ridden prominently by William Buick and although the colt's action suggests he would enjoy fast ground, he had the field off the bridle some way out and then stretched clear in the final furlong to break his maiden. Despite him hitting the line hard, six furlongs could well be his trip next year and on fast ground he could be one to keep onside of, especially with his size, scope and pedigree which suggests he has lots more to offer over the sprinting trips as a 3-year-old.

# Calyx

b c Kingman - Helleborine (Observatory)

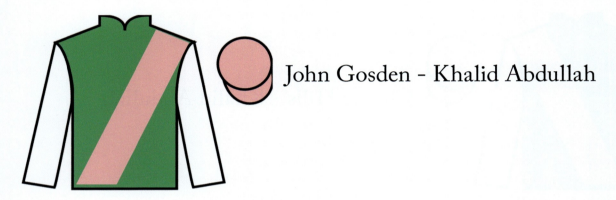

John Gosden - Khalid Abdullah

**Calyx** gave Kingman his first win as a sire when he disposed of his opposition on debut at Newmarket making little fuss of the terrain, recording a timeform rating up there with Frankel's for a debut run. He possesses a wicked turn of foot like his sire. The colt was then turned over quickly to run in the Coventry Stakes at Royal Ascot, that move in itself shows the confidence John Gosden has in the ability of Calyx. He pulled seven lengths clear of his side of the field and raced by himself to win the Coventry in a quick time; for a two-year-old to be capable of this on a stage such as Royal Ascot, ten days after his debut takes some ability and horse. Making him a live contender for the 2,000 Guineas or wherever he goes next year. A top-class colt who Gosden is keen will get a mile and is a Guineas horse.

# Cap Francais

b c Frankel – Miss Cap Ferrat (Darshaan)

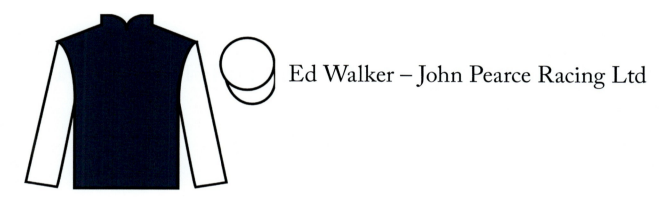

Ed Walker – John Pearce Racing Ltd

**Cap Francais** made an encouraging debut at Newbury, staying on nicely to finish second but showed plenty of inexperience. Reappearing at Salisbury, he justified favouritism and despite showing signs of greenness, produced some class to pull clear in the final furlong. The colt is a nice type and though he isn't the biggest physically, he hits the line hard and is bred to be useful. His third start was very impressive, where he took on some notable types in a hot novice at Haydock; winning comfortably by 2¼ lengths. The Frankel colt is improving upon every run, if he can continue this rate of progression next season, along with a strengthening time away from racing; the colt could be a top prospect for Ed Walker.

## Casanova

b c Frankel – Karen's Caper (War Chant)

John Gosden – HRH Princess Haya Of Jordan

**Casanova** surrendered a number of lengths on debut when dwelling in the stalls at Wolverhampton. The colt was shaken up to retrieve the lost ground but despite this stayed on impressively from the back of the field to finish a flying fourth. Gosden trained his dam and being a Frankel, the mile should suit him. Although his pedigree suggests the mile will be his optimum trip, Frankel progeny tend to be useful over middle distance and his debut performance implies he could make the step up in trip. The well-bred colt could be a useful type in 2019.

# Chairmanoftheboard

b c Slade Power – Bound Copy (Street Cry)

Mick Channon – David Kilburn, David Hudd & Chris Wright

Mick Channon looks to have a good one on his hands and this Slade Power colt justified even money favouritism on debut on soft ground at Goodwood by bolting up. Held in high regard, **Chairmanoftheboard** holds an entry for the Irish 2,000 Guineas and was picked up for just 27,000gns at the October Tattersalls Book 2. Travelling smoothly into contention, the colt made lightwork of the field on debut and once understanding what was asked of him pulled eight lengths of a 79 rated horse in Sir Busker, who was three and a half lengths clear of the following pack. Interestingly, he re-found the bridle in the final furlong and from this evidence, the colt will be racing further than the six furlongs he made his debut at. He could be anything and is one to keep onside of, especially in the armoury of Mick Channon. Whatever level he is he will win races next season.

# Dubai Beauty

b f Frankel – Minidress (Street Cry)

Saeed Bin Suroor – Godolphin

The daughter of Frankel battled well and stayed on nicely to make her debut a winning one. She then went to the May Hill, where she was well backed but disappointed when hitting the front and was soon headed, finishing seventh of eleven. Despite that performance I wouldn't give up on the half-sister to Petticoat and believe she will be an interesting type looking into 2019, especially if she was stepped up in trip. Even on debut, although she did it comfortably in the end, it took the filly some time to finally get on top of her counterpart. The same can be said for her May Hill performance where she was asked to quickened; just not having the change of gears to finish off the race. Saeed Bin Suroor has been well over-due a good one and this beautifully bred filly looks way too big for the Oaks (50/1), a trip which should suit her well.

# East

ch f Frankel – Vital Statistics (Indian Ridge)

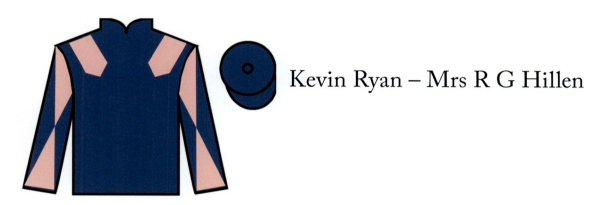

Kevin Ryan – Mrs R G Hillen

**East** was a winner on debut for Kevin Ryan at Hamilton leaving some useful types in behind her. *Happy Power* particularly, who came out and solidified the form when landing a gamble at the Futurity Trophy meeting at Doncaster. An expensive purchase at the Gorsesbirdge Breeze Up, where she was visually very impressive and her sale justified that; selling for €315,000. The daughter of Frankel was then stepped up in trip and class, sent over to Saint-Cloud for the Group 3 Prix Thomas Byron Jockey Club. Here she travelled strongly and once she found her stride, stretched away from the field; a nice opening for the filly found by trainer Kevin Ryan. He looks to have a progressive and straightforward filly who may appreciate the step up to a mile in 2019.

# Fabriano

b c Sinndar – Four Roses (Darshaan)

Roger Varian – Sheikh Mohammed
Obaid Al Maktoum

**Fabriano** ran well on debut at Haydock when finishing fifth of eleven runners on good to soft ground. The colt was held up and made strong headway towards the finish. If it wasn't for being halted he would've surely finished a lot closer. Sinndar progeny tend to progress from their juvenile careers; the colt has all the components to be a useful type next year over an extended trip. A brother to a Blindford Stakes winning filly Fours Sins, out of an unraced French Derby winning sired mare, **Fabriano** is bred to enjoy middle distance and should be competitive in the coming year. The Derby entry also strengthens the colt's claims.

# Fairyland

b f Kodiac – Queenofthefairies (Pivotal)

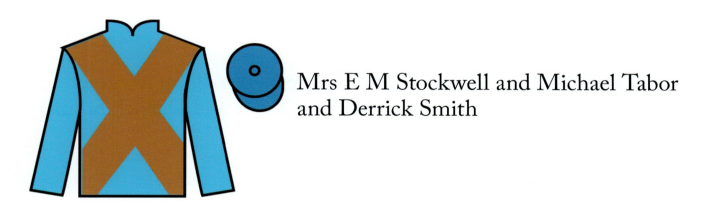

Mrs E M Stockwell and Michael Tabor and Derrick Smith

A Group 1 and Group 2 winner in her 2-year-old campaign; **Fairyland** confirmed the form with *The Mackem Bullet*. Taking the Cheveley Park Stakes by a head, having previously beaten the same opponent a nose in the Lowther Stakes. The Kodiac filly is a progressive type that has only raced on good to firm ground, being out of a Pivotal mare and observing her action, the filly looks fairly versatile ground wise. She possesses plenty of speed and finishes off her races strongly, her performances suggest she could step up in trip and if she were to compete over a mile would demand respect.

# Fleeting

b f Zoffany – Azafata (Motivator)

Aiden O'Brien – Mrs John Magnier and Michael Tabor and Derrick Smith

**Fleeting** was a convincing winner of the May Hill Stakes at Doncaster; she was held up and picked off the leaders in some style to land the Group 2. The filly was trialled over six furlongs in the Grangecon Stakes after breaking her maiden on debut. The trip didn't suit and she was soon outpaced and passed by some speedier rivals, finishing last of seven. The Zoffany filly was then stepped back up in trip to a mile, which she relished and has put in good performances at Group 2 & Group 3 level. Motivator progeny tend to progress from their juvenile careers and an Aiden O'Brien winner on debut too, makes **Fleeting** a filly to respect in 2019.

Just Wonderful – A filly with bundles of potential for A. O'Brien

# G-J

## Gentile Bellini

b c Dubawi – Sky Lantern (Red Clubs)

Aiden O'Brien – Derrick Smith, Mrs John Magnier and Michael Tabor

An interesting recruit to the Aiden O'Brien yard, an expensive purchase at 2,000,000gns he is from a successful family and the price tag can be justified. The pedigree not one you would usually associate with O'Brien and these owners; the colt being out of Richard Hannon trained Guineas and Group 1 winning filly Sky Lantern and covered by Godolphin's Dubawi. Finishing fourth at Leopardstown on debut he will come on a lot from the run and shaped as though he'll stay further than the mile he debuted at. Most of his best work was done in the final furlong. A fascinating colt for the O'Brien team and one that looks like he could be very useful over middle distance next year.

# Ghaiyyath

ch c Dubawi – Nightime (Galileo)

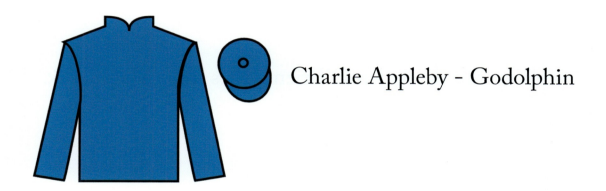

Charlie Appleby - Godolphin

**Ghaiyyath** suffered an unfortunate injury which ruled him out for the majority of his promising 3-year-old career. This caused the colt to miss the Derby and St. Leger classics, which were sure to suit. The son of Dubawi stays strongly and holds some interesting form from his juvenile campaign. He is now entering his 4-year-old career but with such a limited racing as a 3-years-old, he fits in perfectly. Appearing late in the season to take the Prix du Prince d'Orange Group 3, supports that his injuries are behind him. Out of the Irish 1,000 Guineas winning Galileo filly Nightime. A daughter of the mare, Zhukova trained on successfully as a 4-year-old and 5-year-old, suggests that Ghaiyyath could replicate his half-sister and progress with age. A colt with plenty of potential and one that can make up for lost time.

## Goddess

b f Camelot - Cherry Hinton (Green Desert)

Aiden O'Brien - Mrs John Magnier & John G Sikura

**Goddess** – beautifully named and bred, she was involved in a typical Curragh race on debut where she was hampered badly and eased up after suffering a coming together, finishing ninth of twelve.. On reappearance she went off a short price favourite for a small field maiden and recorded a ten length winning margin, where she looked very impressive. Following up from this she was turned over in a Group 3, where she didn't have it all her own way and was again eased out of contention, this time by Ryan Moore. Obviously a very talented filly but large fields and competitiveness seems to throw her off her game, for this backing her for an Oaks or a Guineas may be implausible, but hopefully Aiden O'Brien and the team can find her a nice opening and get the daughter of Camelot some black type in smaller fields where she can have her own way.

# Gossamer Wings

b f Scat Daddy – Lavender Baby (Rubiano)

Aiden O'Brien – Derrick Smith, Mrs John Magnier and Michael Tabor

A filly who travels strongly over five furlongs and has plenty of speed. The well-bred **Gossamer Wings** is not one to give up on, with a drop back to the minimum distance suiting. All of her best performances have come over the five furlongs, and interestingly her poorer performances coming over the furlong further. Trialled at five furlongs on debut she missed the break but learn a lot from that. The filly of the late Scat Daddy travelled like the winner in the Queen Mary (five furlongs, Group 2) but was collared by Signora Cabello. She followed up by disappointing over the 6f in the Duchess of Cambridge Stakes, when not staying the trip. A filly with a lot of potential and ability that is best used at the minimum trip, first-time blinkers tried in the Cheveley Park Stakes (six furlongs); the only mishap with this horse is the distance.

# Grandmaster Flash

ch c Australia – Kittens (Marju)

Joseph Patrick O'Brien – LECH Racing Limited

A colt by Australia with a Derby entry for trainer Joseph O'Brien. **Grandmaster Flash** was beaten on debut by another promising colt with an Irish 2,000 Guineas entry, these two pulled six lengths clear of the third, who looks a useful type too. Racing in mid-division, Grandmaster Flash made up ground to challenge the eventual winner. *Thebeastfortheeast* made all the running and held on gamely; a colt held in very high regard by Richard O'Brien. Joseph O'Brien's colt took some pulling up after the line, shaping as though he will enjoy a step up in trip. Middle distance should suit him next season and he could be very useful, despite being picked up for only 52,000gns as a yearling.

# Handmaiden

b f Invincible Spirit - Zabeel Park (Medicean)

John Gosden – HH Sheikha Al Jalila Racing

She was a debut second behind highly-rated juvenile Quorto who has since come out and recorded Group 1 & 2 victories. From that run, **Handmaiden** swapped the Godolphin blue for the former Godolphin silks and is now owned by HH Sheikha Al Jalila Racing. She was backed on the day of her second run as if defeat was not an option, Godolphin filly Lover's Knot drifted in the market but managed to get back up to head the filly on the line. **Handmaiden** should make into an interesting type over a mile next year with her pedigree based around seven furlongs to a mile being a half-sister to Group 1 winners. She has disappointed on her reappearance but isn't a filly to give up on, hopefully she will come on from her juvenile career.

# Hermosa

b f Galileo – Beauty Is Truth (Pivotal)

Aiden O'Brien – Derrick Smith, Mrs John Magnier and Michael Tabor

A pedigree that Aiden O'Brien is familiar with, **Hermosa** is a full sister to the Group 1 winning Hydrangea and being by the Pivtoal mare it seems as though she's fairly versatile ground wise. She enjoys the mile and was unfortunate not to land her first Group 1 in a strange renewal of the Fillies' Mile. Improving upon every run she has she could make into a very nice prospect next year for Aiden O'Brien. She could well be programmed similarly to her sister, Hydrangea. She has already taken a similar route thus far in her career.

# Hidden Message

bb f Scat Daddy – Secret Charm (Green Desert)

William Haggas – Qatar Racing Limited

An interesting filly for William Haggas and Qatar Racing, the daughter of Scat Daddy made her debut at Yarmouth over six furlongs and was well backed into favouritism. The filly was given a couple shakes of the reins when travelling strongly into the contest and quickened readily to run out a 3¾ length winner. Visually she has a lot of scope for a filly so has room for improvement and will be given plenty of time to prepare for races. She should be found a nice couple of races next year and be difficult to stop, especially if she improves and fills into her frame over the winter.

# Jack's Point

b c Slade Power – Electra Star (Shamardal)

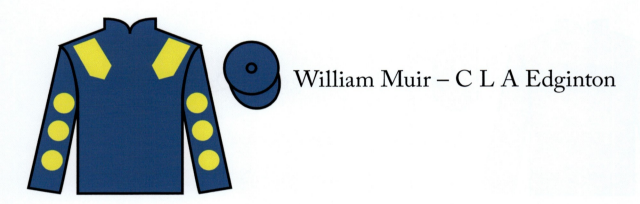

William Muir – C L A Edginton

An interesting juvenile that caught the eye for William Muir and one which is held in high regard. **Jack's Point** ran well behind some useful types on both starts at Newmarket followed by the colt recording a win of his own at Chelmsford in a competitive four-runner Plus-10 Race. He seemed to handle the AW and despite the bump at the start of the race held on gamily to win by a neck. Out of a useful family and has tremendous scope for a 2-year-old. The 120,000g yearling should be full of improvement for the Muir yard and looks to be one to keep onside of for 2019.

# Japan

b c Galileo – Shastye (Danehill)

Aiden O'Brien – Derrick Smith and Mrs John Magnier and Michael

**Japan** is a progressive type for Aiden O'Brien. Finishing seventh on debut, he learnt plenty and reappeared to win on heavy ground at Listowel. The sharpness of Listowel's trip didn't suit the Galileo colt but once he found his rhythm in the straight, he stayed on strongly – making up a number of lengths – to break his maiden by a head. The colt boasts tremendous stamina and is a hardened, typical son of Galileo. He should be a very useful prospect over middle distance next year. Despite showing signs of greenness, he took the Beresford Stakes at Naas, emphasizing that improvement in the full brother to Sir Isaac Newton is still possible.

# Jash

b c Kodiac – Miss Azeza (Dutch Art)

Simon Crisford – Hamdan Al Maktoum

A smart prospect for Simon Crisford winning impressively on debut at Newmarket, going off a hot favourite. He travelled strongly and once he went through the gears pulled away nicely from the field. The Kodiac colt has a lot of speed and an exciting turn of foot, his optimum trip is unknown as his pedigree suggests six/seven furlongs will be his prime distances. **Jash** was held by Ten Sovereigns in the Middle Park when thrown up to Group 1 class, the unbeaten pair pulled three lengths clear of the field and looked two very promising horses for next season, putting up an excellent time at Newmarket. A horse which should prove difficult to beat, if he is found some nice openings next season.

# Just Wonderful

b f Dansili – Wading (Montjeu)

Aiden O'Brien – Derrick Smith, Mrs John Magnier and Michael Tabor

**Just Wonderful** was a winner on debut for the O'Brien team and any Aiden O'Brien horse that comes out and wins first time out warrants respect. Out of the lightly raced Group 2 winning Ballydoyle filly Wading, closely related to Sea the Stars and a half-sister to Galileo, the filly is bred to be great and is well thought of by the O'Brien team holding Breeder's Cup and 1000 Guineas entries. She reversed the form with Main Edition when winning the Rockfel Stakes at Newmarket in nice fashion, she travels well and enjoys picking off races from off the pace. A filly with bundles of ability and one that could make up into a potentially classy three-year-old.

Persian King & Magna Grecia – Two promising colts for 2019

# K-Q

# Kadar

bb c Scat Daddy -Kaloura (Sinndar)

Karl Burke – Phoenix Thoroughbred Limited

The Karl Burke trained son of Scat Daddy looked promising when being heavily backed on debut and turning over Gosden's 4/7 favourite Waldstern, who on debut looked a promising individual himself. It took the colt plenty of time to find an opening, but once he did he began to pull away from the field. Burke was keen on the horse's chance before the race. When a trainer like Burke says he'll be competitive in a Guineas you have to sit up and take note. Being out of a Sinndar mare, on pedigree it looks as though he has every chance of staying – Sinndar being an Arc and Derby winner – Burke is confident the colt will be racing at middle distance next year. Also quoting he wouldn't mind soft ground. Being a Scat Daddy, it is unusual but from the evidence we've seen so far you wouldn't be surprised if he went for the Derby (40/1), especially as Sinndar's progeny usually come on from their juvenile season and have their best year of racing at three. Regally bred; major prospect.

# Lady Kaya

b f Dandy Man – Kayak (Singspiel)

Ms Sheila Lavery – Joanne Lavery

A useful filly who shaped well on debut when finishing third, in a trio that pulled clear of the rest of the field. She then made all in her next start in a strangely run race which saw her eight lengths clear, three furlongs in. She recorded an impressive ten-length win in the end, Pink Dogwood coming out and winning convincingly bolstered the form. **Lady Kaya** reappeared bumping into nice type Skitter Skatter in her next two runs, contesting Group 1 and Group 2 level races. She looked the winner some way out in the Molygare before Skitter Skatter found her feet up the hill and pulled away. She is a filly with a lot of nice entries, and she should be suited by a step up in trip and found a nice couple of openings in 2019.

# Legends of War

b c Scat Daddy - Madera Dancer (Rahy)

John Gosden - Qatar Racing Limited

A colt that hit the ground running when recording an impressive win on debut at Yarmouth. Visually emphatic he jumped into the trackers of many. Although the colt hasn't lived up to expectations nor the form working out as good as people thought it might, the son of Scat Daddy has still impressed and a couple of runs of his can be excused. **Legends of War** possesses a useful turn of foot. The head win at 1/4 favouritism at Newbury was a 3-runner race and he was asked to make the running himself down the centre of the track, he also didn't get the run of the race in the July Stakes; a colt that would be very interesting once upped to 6f. He could make a very nice 3-year-old for the season and one not give up on. Quick ground being his optimum conditions.

# Line of Duty

ch c Galileo – Jacqueline Quest (Rock of Gibraltar)

Charlie Appleby - Godolphin

**Line of Duty** relished the step up in trip from seven furlongs to a mile, after his first two starts saw him defeated by some sharper opponents. On debut, **Line of Duty** found little room to race and was switched deep inside the final furlong. He made eye-catching headway only to be denied by a head. He then reappeared at Haydock going off a short price favourite but found the speedy and highly regarded Great Scot one too good. The Galileo colt stays strongly and finds plenty under pressure. Stepping up in trip and class, he bravely took the Prix de Conde, showing a nice turn of foot to move through a gap; battling off the useful Frankel colt Syrtis. After hitting the line hard on all of his starts, he should appreciate the step up in trip and be an interesting type over middle-distance next year, with the Derby trip sure to suit.

# Madhmoon

b c Dawn Approach – Aaraas (Haafhd)

Kevin Prendergast – Hamdan Al Maktoum

An exciting prospect for Kevin Prendergast and owner Hamdan Al Maktoum. The latter has been well overdue a classic winner and has a live chance with **Madhmoon**. The colt quickened up on debut to leave some useful types behind him including Aiden O'Brien's subsequent winners: Sydney Opera House, Constantinople and Broome. **Madhmoon** followed up on his next appearance, when stepping up in class for the Champion Juvenile stakes and recording another impressive victory. He looks a strong and powerful son of Dawn Approach and one that travels strikingly into races whilst possessing a nice turn of foot, which has put his first two starts to bed. Held in high regard by Prendergast, who has trained one or two in his fifty-five years in the game. He will be competitive in the Guineas and any Group race that he shows up to next season, warrants plenty of respect.

# Magna Grecia

b c Invincible Spirit - Cabaret (Galileo)

Aiden O'Brien – D Smith & Mrs J Magnier & M Tabor & Flaxman Stables Ireland

He strode clear on debut at Naas to record a 3½ length victory over some stoutly bred opponents. **Magna Grecia** looks a strong and powerful type, held in high regard at Ballydoyle. He looks to be the spearhead of O'Brien's Futurity Trophy (Group 1, Doncaster) bid though quoted he may go for the Killavullan (Group 3, Leopardstown). It wouldn't be surprising if he skipped the Killavullan as he looks to have his sights aimed higher. The colt looks classy and is still learning and improving, to win on debut for a yard like O'Brien's – who's tend to come on for the run – is promising and suggests the Invincible Spirit colt could be anything and is a serious player next year.

# Mallacoota

b f Australia – Mauralakana (Muhathir)

Mrs John Harrington–R Scarborough

**Mallacoota** shaped well on debut when staying on to finish tenth of twenty in a hot maiden race, she made some nice headway but encountered traffic which halted her progress. The daughter of Australia was then dropped in trip from a mile to seven furlongs, reappearing at Leopardstown. Here she attempted to make all the running but was headed in the final furlong, despite running encouragingly and showing a lovely action. Although she was dropped back to seven furlongs, the filly stayed on well and a return back to a mile or further will suit. **Mallacoota** is from an interesting family, being by Australia and her performances thus far suggest she has all the components to make into a nice 3-year-old and a versatile one trip wise.

# Maydanny

b c Dubawi – Attraction (Efisio)

Mark Johnston – Hamdan Al Maktoum

Mark Johnston trained Guineas hope Elarqam for Hamdan Al Maktoum, a horse which showed plenty of potential as a juvenile but didn't progress as a three-year-old. His unraced half-brother **Maydanny** was an expensive purchase, alike Elarqam, costing 1,350,000gns at the Tattersalls Book 1. The pedigree is fascinating; Attraction, a 5-time Group 1 winning filly and despite her irregular action possessed plenty of speed. Covered by Dubawi, a more compact and robust type, whose progeny stay the mile well and physically are impressive. The pedigree is capable of building a talented performer. **Maydanny** holds a Derby entry and although he hasn't been given his debut yet he could be a top prospect based upon connections.

# Norway

b c Galileo – Love Me True (Kingmambo)

Aiden O'Brien – Derrick Smith, Mrs John Magnier and Michael Tabor

**Norway** is still a maiden for Aiden O'Brien, the Galileo colt is screaming for a step up in trip. Shaping well on both starts but not having the turn of foot to compete in the final furlong, staying on well. Shaped and races similarly to St. Leger winner Kew Gardens, he has been campaigned at seven furlongs and then a mile. The team recognise this horse will stay and should be winning races over further than a mile in the future. A half brother to Ruler of The World and Duke of Marmalade, who both won Group 1s over the middle distance. Duke of Marmalade being the sire of Big Orange, Simple Verse and Marmelo emphasises that staying ability that is in **Norway's** pedigree. The colt could progress and the St. Leger trip and conditions look to suit him. (33/1)

# Persian King

b c Kingman – Pretty Please (Dylan Thomas)

Andre Fabre - Ballymore Thoroughbred Ltd

A colt with huge scope and potential for Andre Fabre, he has made lightwork of the fields at Chantilly on his last two starts over a mile and looks as though he could be anything. The colt visually showing signs of greenness could mean he has a lot more to offer. Fabre is keen on the Kingman colt and described him as his best juvenile. He will probably want fast ground by the look of his action, and could make the journey over for the 2,000 Guineas rather than the French equivalent. The most striking thing about the colt is his size, he dwarfed the field on his previous start when going off 3/5 favourite and although we don't know what he has beaten he looked almightily impressive. An unknown quantity which is worth respecting and keeping onside from a powerful stable.

# Pretty Pollyanna

b f Oasis Dream – Unex Mona Lisa (Shamardal)

Michael Bell - W J and T C O Gredley

Michael Bell's filly has been at the head of the 1,000 Guineas market for a persistent amount of time and she is a worthy favourite. Her most impressive performance being the Prix L'Morny where she battled off Signora Cabello to win her first Group 1 in a time .56 quicker than standard; the filly has bundles of speed and she seems straightforward type. Although on pedigree you could make a case for her staying the mile, her performances when stepped up in trip have seen her out-stayed. If the Oasis Dream filly can stay the mile then she is a real contender for the Guineas, nevertheless Bell has a very talented filly at his disposal and one that should be exciting moving into the 2019 season.

# Quorto

b c Dubawi - Volume (Mount Nelson)

Charlie Appleby - Godolphin

**Quorto** didn't go unbacked on his first two starts as a juvenile. He ran out an impressive winner of the Superlative Stakes beating O'Brien colt Cape of Good Hope three and a quarter lengths and despite showing signs of greenness ran on well and finished strongly at Newmarket over seven furlongs. This performance showed a step up in trip would benefit the colt and ground wise, his action looks very versatile and a bit of cut probably wouldn't go amiss. The greenness suggests he has further improvement in him and if he settles could get a mile or more comfortably and be very good. He came out to win impressively in the Group 1 National Stakes beating Anthony Van Dyck. Quorto had everything in his favour; a 7f trip and cut in the ground allowed him to show his class over an O'Brien colt, who probably wanted further but put up an intriguing battle.

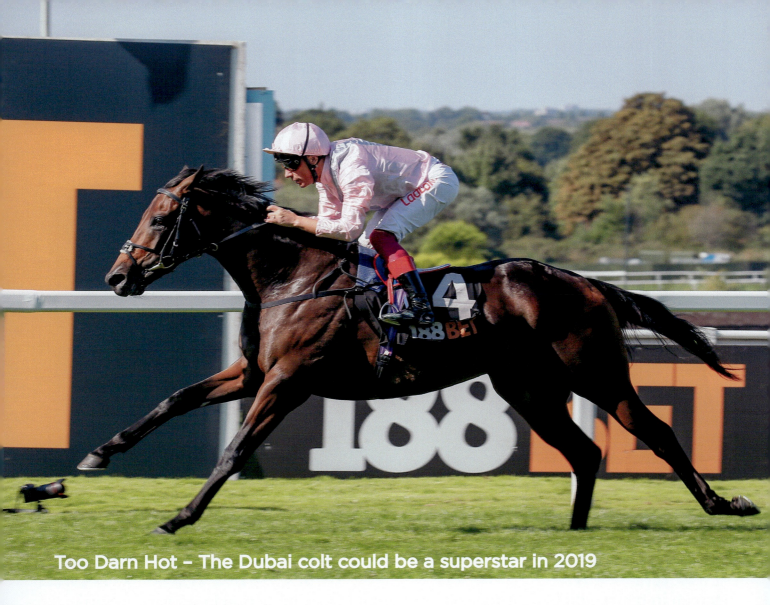

Too Darn Hot – The Dubai colt could be a superstar in 2019

# R-Z

# Rainbow Heart

b f Born to Sea – Sea of Heartbreak (Rock of Gibraltar)

William Haggas – Sunderland Holding Inc

**Rainbow Heart** is an interesting filly for William Haggas and the Sea of Class owners Sunderland Holding Inc. The filly stayed on well to finish third on debut despite being switched for a run inside the final furlongs. Reappearing at Newmarket she went off a short price favourite, where the daughter of Born to Sea won comfortably by nine lengths. She is well bred and her pedigree is based around 1m-1m2f, Haggas quoted she will go for the Oak trials and start off over a mile in 2019. **Rainbow Heart** could be anything and her potential is still unknown, from the two performances, we have seen and considering the connections, she deserves respect.

# Rakan

b c Sea the Stars – Tarfasha (Teofilo)

Dermot Weld – Hamdan Al Maktoum

**Rakan** is a fascinatingly bred colt of Sea the Stars. His dam was also trained by Dermot Weld, winning the Blandford Stakes and finishing second in the Epsom Oaks for Hamdan Al Maktoum. His pedigree suggests he should be a useful performer at middle distance next year and with a Derby entry the colt must be respected, especially with confidence in the likelihood of improvement. He then progressed nicely from his debut to win at Leopardstown next time out, breaking his maiden in a competitive field. **Rakan** travelled strongly and displayed a nice action; tracking the leaders before then being shaken up and extending nicely away from the field.

# Red Impression

g f Dark Angel – Purissima (Fusaichi Pegasus)

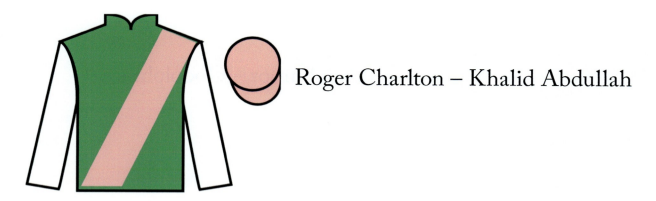

Roger Charlton – Khalid Abdullah

An unbeaten filly for Roger Charlton and Khalid Abdullah, the daughter of Dark Angel has shown a nice turn of foot on her first two starts to record two comfortable wins. **Red Impression** is now two from two after disposing of the field at Lingfield, tracking the leader before lengthening and extending to record a six-length victory. The time she recorded at Lingfield was impressive, a progression from the filly's first run and if this grey daughter of Dark Angel was to continue to improve, would be a top prospect. Being a close relative to the Bobby Frankel trained Group 1 winner Etoule Montante, who did most of her racing over seven furlongs to a mile, suggests she could be performing at further than six furlongs. However, she is a filly with a lot of speed and this could prove her most effective distance.

## Royal Meeting

b c Invincible Spirit – Rock Opera (Lecture)

Saeed Bin Suroor – Godolphin

**Royal Meeting** was heavily backed on debut at Yarmouth and made up plenty of ground to get up and win going away from a competitive field. He holds an entry for the Irish 2,000 Guineas and is a colt that possesses a lot speed, Rock Opera being a Grade 1 winning mare over six furlongs in South Africa and having been covered by Invincible Spirit has yet more speed in inheritance. The colt still has to grow into his frame and would've learnt a lot from the win at Yarmouth in September. Bin Suroor quoted that Oisin Murphy liked the colt and that he was "Listed level plus" for next year. One to keep on side of for 2019 especially if he fills into his frame and progresses physically.

# Sangarius

b c Kingman - Trojan Queen (Empire Maker)

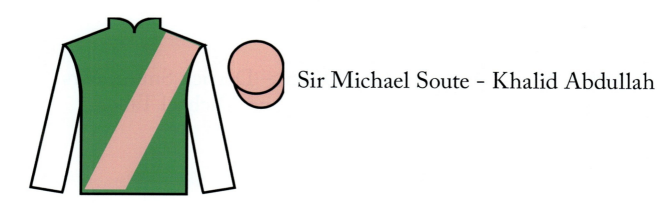

Sir Michael Soute - Khalid Abdullah

**Sangarius** looks a progressive sort and was well backed on debut, going off the 11/8 favourite at Newmarket. He travelled like the winner three furlongs out, switched for a run with confidence under James Doyle inside the two-furlong mark and probably made harder work than seemed necessary. The Sir Michael Stoute trained colt is unbeaten on his first two starts and looks to be improving, responding to pressure from Ryan Moore at listed level during the St Leger meeting. He pulled away from the field and on that evidence would be suited by a step up in trip. The son of Kingman will be a live chance for the 2,000 Guineas (33/1). From all the signs shown so far, this horse could be a very good one for Sir Michael Stoute and Khalid Abdullah.

## Sergei Prokofiev

b c Scat Daddy – Orchard Beach (Tapit)

Aiden O'Brien – Derrick Smith, Mrs John Magnier and Michael Tabor

**Sergei Prokofiev** was all the talk when breaking his maiden at Naas, the son of Scat Daddy soon became the market leader for the Coventry Stakes. Even in his most recent runs he has shown signs of greenness and pulls very hard. The drop back to minimum distance should treat this colt well and is not one to give up on. He travelled strongly in the Coventry but probably given too much to do, bumping into useful sorts Calyx and Advertise who were probably suited by the six furlongs trip. The six furlongs stretches the colt's raw ability and speed and a return back to the minimum distance on a quick surface could rejuvenate him. A colt that is too talented to give up on and hopefully can be campaigned and found a nice opening over the five furlongs.

# Shades of Blue

b f Kodiac - Enjoyable (Verglas)

Clive Cox - Miss A Jones

**Shades of Blue** showed a tremendous turn of foot when bursting through in the final furlong to record a victory on debut. That run saw her beat Queen of Bermuda, who has subsequently won at Group 3 level and ran credibly in other races of similar level; the rest of the form has also worked out very well. Clive Cox's filly by Kodiac then reappeared and was defeated only a head by Signora Cabello in the Queen Mary, where they put up a good time. The form has worked out well with Signora Cabello winning at Group 2 level and running credibly behind Guineas favourite Pretty Pollyanna in the Prix Morny. O'Brien's Scat Daddy duo Gossamer Wings and So Perfect also look interesting types, the latter coming out and winning at Group 3 level. She's an extremely quick filly and the form she boasts is rock solid and she is assuredly in good hands with Clive Cox.

# Sheriffmuir

b c War Front - Lerici (Woodman)

John Gosden - HRH Princess Haya of Jordan

An interesting recruit to the Gosden yard. Sherrifmuir, a son of War Front that cost $995,000 at the sales. He didn't have the most straight forward of debuts at Newbury, being drawn wide and then racing by himself with little cover for the majority of the race. For a two-year-old debut he showed all the right signs and will come on a lot for the run. Frankie Dettori gave him a nice educational ride and rode him out under hands and heels for third. His family, yard and entries suggest he will be winning races in 2019, rated only 73 based on that run (RPR). A colt in the right hands and worth keeping onside of.

# Skitter Skatter

b f Scat Daddy – Dane Street (Street Cry)

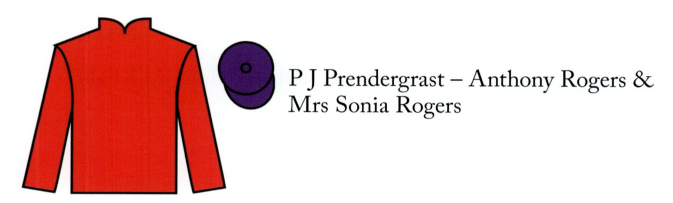

P J Prendergrast – Anthony Rogers & Mrs Sonia Rogers

A beautifully bred filly and one that has to be considered for the 1,000 Guineas (33/1). She broke her maiden at Dundalk, holding off Aiden O'Brien top colt Sergei Prokofiev. **Skitter Skatter** was then stepped up in class for the Fillies Group 3 at Curragh, beaten only a half-length. Building upon that performance she won a Group 3 herself, fending off the Oaks favourite Goddess. Improving upon every run, she progressed to win at Group 1 and Group 2 level including the Molygare Stakes. The daughter of Scat Daddy has an interesting pedigree and her performances suggest she will stay the mile. A nice break now will benefit the filly following a busy but successful juvenile campaign; she is a force to be reckoned with in 2019.

# Stormwave

b c Dalakhani – Celtic Slipper (Anabaa)

Ralph Beckett – Abdulla Al Khalifa

Well fancied on debut at Salisbury, **Stormwave** travelled well, tracking the leaders before making his own effort one furlong out. He saw the trip out well, staying on nicely towards the line. An Interestingly bred colt being a brother to the useful Beckett trained Moonrise Landing who also won on debut. Being by Dalakhani, **Stormwave** should progress nicely from his two-year-old career, the colt has plenty of scope to work into and should return in 2019 a nice type. Ralph Beckett quoting him to be "Very tall and tall but rather backward" suggests the trainer has a lot to work with over the winter. He holds an Irish Derby entry and is held in high regard by Ralph Beckett, based on his performance and with Dalakhani's influence, the colt should be useful over middle distance next year.

# Ten Sovereigns

b c No Nay Never - Seeking Solace (Exceed and Excel)

Aiden O'Brien – Derrick Smith, Mrs John Magnier and Michael Tabor

Major prospect, putting up exciting times and performances on his first starts. This colt hasn't yet been required to showcase his best ability and if he can improve upon what he has shown us he could be very special, especially over the six furlongs. He is bred to be extremely quick out of a son of Scat Daddy, who Aiden O'Brien knows well. By an Exceed and Excel mare, the pedigree has speed in abundance. With his huge frame and scope there is further room for improvement which could make him a major player for sprints in 2019. It would be interesting to see him in a Coventry Stakes at Royal Ascot, as a fast-straight track would suit him. The colt has hit the line hard on both starts, so could certainly be getting the mile next season not necessarily ruling out the Guineas in May.

# Too Darn Hot

b c Dubawi - Dar Re Mi (Singspiel)

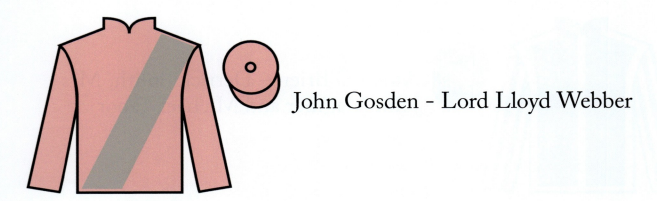

John Gosden - Lord Lloyd Webber

Beautifully bred **Too Darn Hot**, the brother to So Mi Dar and Lah Ti Dar, has been all the rage this year when impressing on all three starts for the Gosden team, and is on everyone's lips for next year's Derby. John Gosden started him over a mile and his family suggests he'll stay the Derby trip, but the Guineas surely looks the best bet (16/1) – the only flaw Gosden already has a hand in the race with Coventry winner Calyx. He's a big scopey colt of Dubawi but still possesses that compact muscular power that his father boasted, he has a smart turn of foot and has had all his races won before the final furlong. If the colt can stay healthy he has the potential to be a superstar.

# Trethias

b f Invincible Spirit – Evita (Selkirk)

Mrs John Harrington – Stonethorn Stud Farms Limited

An interesting filly from the Harrington yard who pulled away eye-catchingly from Aiden O'Brien's Camelot filly Pink Dogwood, who has since herself reappeared winning impressively, a type that also holds entries to some interesting races. **Trethias** was then drawn terribly at Leopardstown, with much of the race her being out the back of the TV, somehow, she managed to finish fourth when staying on from coming wide round the final bend and made impressive late headway. Bred from an interesting family, she is a half-sister to group winners Rewilding and Dar Re Mi, a top filly that is held in high regard and one that should be respected. Hopefully she is found some nice openings and can win races in 2019.

# Turjomaan

bb c War Front – Almoutezah (Storm Cat)

Roger Varian – Hamdan Al Maktoum

Victorious on his first two starts, **Turjomaan** looks a promising colt for Roger Varian. The son of War Front possesses tremendous scope and size for a juvenile, evident in his win at Newcastle. He battled off the second which physically he dwarfed; **Turjomaan** extended away from Wiretap but the pair pulled eight lengths clear of the remainder. By War Front and out of a Storm Cat mare, the colt's optimum conditions will be faster ground and he seemed to handle the AW at Newcastle. The colt also enjoyed the stiffness of the track at both Ascot and Newcastle, as well as the seven furlongs trip. He hits the line hard over the seven furlongs and Andrea Atzeni quoted after his Ascot performance "he will get the mile very well". A physically impressive performer who is an exciting prospect in 2019 for Hamdan Al Maktoum and Roger Varian.

Printed in the United States
By Bookmasters